GARFIELD'S
JUDGMENT DAY

BY: JIM DAVIS

Story by Jim Davis
Adapted by Kim Campbell
Illustrated by
Mike Fentz, Kevin Campbell,
Larry Fentz, Dave Kuhn

BALLANTINE BOOKS • NEW YORK

All rights reserved under International and Pan-American Copyright Conventions.
Published in the United States by Ballantine Books, a division of Random House,
Inc., New York, and simultaneously in Canada by Random House of Canada
Limited, Toronto.

Library of Congress Catalog Card Number: 89-91497

ISBN: 0-345-36755-3

Manufactured in the United States of America

First Edition: July 1990

10   9   8   7   6   5   4   3   2   1

GARFIELD'S

JUDGMENT DAY

Our story begins on a beautiful summer morning. As usual, Garfield is sleeping in his bed, dreaming of lasagna, french fries, chocolate ice cream, and . . . well, you know Garfield. A nice, warm sunbeam finds its way into Garfield's room, signaling him that it is time to get up and have breakfast. Now it is up to Garfield to get Jon out of bed.

With some help from Odie and a few LOUD musical instruments, Jon is soon on his feet and in the kitchen. Garfield orders his usual breakfast of buckwheat pancakes, bacon, eggs benedict, croissants, hash browns, orange juice, coffee . . . and, well, you know Garfield.

Before long, Jon is tired of his energetic pets, who always seem to be underfoot, and they are promptly removed from the kitchen.

A few doors down, the twin toy terriers, Al and Fredo, begin their daily task of stirring the Rossini family to life. The sound of their jingling dog tags and a few well-placed "yips" and "yaps" will do the trick. Al and Fredo leap onto Mr. and Mrs. Rossini's bed, yipping and yapping and jingling their dog tags. The five Rossini children awaken and join Al and Fredo on the bed. Soon there are bouncing pillows, blankets, dogs, and children on the bed.

Down the street from the Rossini house lives old Eli and his faithful companion, Barney. Barney has been in charge of waking Eli every day for the past 18 years. Eli is often grouchy in the morning and today is no exception. Barney walks to his bed and gently nudges Eli.

"Good morning, Barney," says Eli, sweetly. "Thank you for waking me up. I'll bet you'd like some breakfast, wouldn't you?"

Barney nods his head lovingly.

"For 18 years you've been waking me up to get your breakfast. And for 18 years you've been getting your breakfast when I was good and ready to give it to you. Get out of here and let an old man get some sleep!" Eli yelled.

With that, he threw his slipper at Barney. Don't worry about Barney. He knows it's just Eli's way.

Garfield and Odie, you may recall, had been politely asked to remove themselves from the kitchen. While they stood patiently waiting at the back door for Jon to invite them back in, a sudden feeling of dread came over them.

"Something bad is going to happen," thought Garfield. He trembled. A quick survey of the other neighborhood animals revealed that they, too, felt the same uneasiness.

Garfield and Odie were frightened. They wanted to run and hide under Jon's bed along with the dust balls and bunny slippers.

"Let us in, Jon. Please, oh please, oh please! Let us in!" they begged.

Finally, Jon opened the door. They were relieved to be inside, but the feeling of gloom hung on. They ate silently and Garfield didn't even try to steal Odie's food. (Okay, he did, but he didn't enjoy it very much.)

After breakfast, Jon announced he was going to the supermarket. He told Garfield and Odie he'd bring back a surprise. The idea of a surprise brightened them for a moment. Garfield hoped the surprise would be something good to eat.

The time had come for Garfield and Odie to attend their weekly meeting. They started toward the old abandoned theater where they met every Wednesday with Al, Fredo, Barney, Arlene and all the other neighborhood cats and dogs. Sometimes even the stray cats and dogs came. They liked to get together and discuss their problems. There was usually plenty to discuss.

At the theater, the pets were filing through the door. The usual conversations were taking place.

"Wet!"

"Dry!"

"Wet, I say!"

"I prefer dry!"

While a couple of cats argued over which was better, wet or dry cat food, Jacob and Rover discussed their flea problems. Three stray dogs named Lorenzo, Willard, and Bob roamed in off the street. As usual, they, too, were arguing. Willard liked to think he was the leader of the three, and that suited Lorenzo and Bob just fine.

Eventually Jacob called the meeting to order. Jacob was a distinguished dog, well-liked and respected by the other pets. The first item of business was what to do about the Wilson family. Seems they had just had their poor little kitten, Mittens, declawed. It was agreed that the Wilsons should be punished, so Lorenzo, Willard and Bob volunteered to knock over their trash cans. Lorenzo, Willard and Bob were not the most reliable or well-respected dogs, but they were good at knocking down trash cans, chasing mailmen, digging up flower beds, and other favorite cat and dog pranks.

Next, the discussion turned to the pets's anger over all the stupid names they had been given. There were a lot of unhappy cats named "Muffin" and all the dogs in the crowd who had been born with a spot, were naturally named "Spot". (All the spotted dogs except Odie, that is.)

At about that time, a mouse scrambled out of its hole, making a daring attempt to cross the theater. All the cats immediately tore out of their seats in hot pursuit of the brave mouse. Jacob tried to regain control of the meeting, but when he could see his efforts were useless, he threw his paws up in disgust and the meeting was adjourned.

"Wait!" yelled Garfield. "This meeting is not adjourned!"

The theater became silent and all eyes were on Garfield.

"I sensed something bad coming our way. Odie does, too! Admit it—don't all of you feel it?" asked Garfield.

A quick scan of the crowd revealed that, indeed, all the animals felt the same uneasiness.

"There's a storm coming that will destroy this town. We'll be lucky to survive. And what about our owners? They're our responsibility. They are also our food, our shelter, and our friends. We've got to warn them! My owner isn't great, but I'd sure hate to break in a new one at this late date," Garfield exclaimed.

A dog in the crowd asked, "What are we supposed to do about it, Garfield?"

"Face it!" cried Garfield. "It's judgment day, people. We must warn our owners now and bring them to the safety of this old theater. The walls are three feet thick, and there's no way this baby will blow. And, here's the really great thing. There's only one way to do it: we tell them."

The crowd of cats and dogs looked shocked as Garfield began to move his lips. He was speaking the way humans do.

"Come on, everyone. Now's your chance to be a hero."

"We can't. We have a pact with the other cats and dogs of the world. We swore we'd never speak to humans. We can't break the pact!" said a cat named Muffin.

Garfield argued that the wrath of the storm would be much worse than the wrath of the other pets of the world.

"Besides," Garfield said, "we'll just make it through the storm and then stop talking and pretend the whole thing never happened. Okay?! Who's with me?"

There was silence in the old theater for a moment and then Arlene, Garfield's faithful friend, spoke, moving her lips like Garfield had just done.

"I'm with you, Garfield."

There was a gasp in the audience, but once Arlene had broken the ice, the other pets began to try their voices, too. Soon, there was singing and yelling and laughter mixed in with catcalls and barking.

Garfield was curious about what Odie's voice would sound like, but when he asked Odie to "speak", Odie just barked.

"Somehow, Ol' Boy, I'm not surprised."

When they finally tired of hearing their own voices, the pets left the theater. They had a tremendous task before them . . . to convince their owners a storm was coming and get them to shelter immediately.

Back at Barney's house, his owner Eli sat in his favorite old rocking chair fast asleep. Barney nudged Eli.

Eli snorted and asked, "What is it, Barney?"

"I have something to tell you, Eli."

"You're doggone right you have something to tell me, you ol' reprobate . . . I'm dead, right?"

Barney chuckled. "No, you old fool. There's a terrible storm coming. We've got to get to shelter right now."

Somehow, Eli didn't seem surprised that Barney could talk.

"I always knew you could talk, you flea-bitten hunk of buzzard bait. How's come you waited 'til now to speak up?"

Barney tried to explain to Eli just how serious the storm was, but Eli was more interested in talking to his old companion than he was in hearing about the storm.

In a dark and dirty alley, several blocks from the theater, Arlene approached her home. Arlene's home did not have a fence around it. Arlene's home did not have a yard, a tree, or a flower. Arlene's home didn't even have windows. Arlene lived in a box. She didn't have an owner to warn. Arlene was a stray.

Arlene was ashamed of this fact. It was a secret she had kept for many years. Not even her good friend, Garfield, knew she was a stray.

Most of the cats and the dogs in the neighborhood looked down on stray animals. Arlene was afraid she'd lose her friends if they knew she was an alley cat.

Back at the Rossini house, Al and Fredo darted into the room where Angelo sat reading the newspaper.

"Angelo, Angelo! Listen to us! A storm's coming, a storm's coming! We gotta get out of here! Run! Run! Grab the kids! Grab the wife! A storm's coming!" yipped Al and Fredo.

Angelo lowered his paper.

"Shut up, you dogs. Go play outside. Never a moment's peace. The wife . . . she talk all the time. The kids . . . they talk all the time. The dogs . . . they talk, talk, talk . . ."

Suddenly, Angelo realized what he was saying.

"My nimanamwawa," Angelo muttered.

"Lunch!" shouted Gina Rossini from the kitchen.

"My nimanamwawa," Angelo repeated.

"Angelo, you not making sense. What you saying?" asked Gina. "Come out here and eat your lunch."

A stampede of screaming children raced through the room. Angelo sat in a stupor, mumbling to himself.

"Mama, Mama!" cried the children. "The dogs! They talk! There's a storm coming! We gotta run! Come on, Mama. Come on, Pap! Al and Fredo can talk!" cried the children.

"Mama mia! The dogs! They talk?! What storm? Where? Mama mia! Run! Run!" Gina ran screaming from the kitchen with the children and dogs following closely behind. Angelo just sat in his chair, too stunned to move.

Jon was in the kitchen unloading groceries when Garfield and Odie arrived home.

"Hi, boys. Remember the surprise I promised you?" said Jon in his usual friendly manner. "Don't you just love surprises?"

"Yes, we do," replied Garfield. "Do you?"

THUMP! Jon fainted and fell in a heap on the floor.

Several minutes later, Jon recovered and sat up.

"Garfield! I can't believe you're actually talking to me," exclaimed Jon. "Am I dreaming? Am I crazy?"

Garfield just nodded.

"Can Odie talk, too?" asked Jon in amazement.

Odie just barked and ran in circles. Jon continued to question Garfield.

"I have a million questions for you. Like . . . what's it like to have four legs?"

"Confusing. Now listen, Jon. You've got to get out of the house. There's a . . ."

"Can you really see in the dark?" interrupted Jon.

"Yes. With a flashlight. Now listen . . ."

"How do you make that purring sound?" Jon asked.

Garfield grabbed Jon by the collar. "When we get to the theater, I'll tell you anything you want to know. Now come on!"

"Can all animals talk?"

"LET'S GO!" screamed Garfield.

At Eli's house, the room darkened as the sun was swallowed by a dark cloud. The wind began to howl and Eli's rickety old house started creaking as the wind ripped through the neighborhood.

"I'm not going," Eli said stubbornly.

"Do you hear that wind, you old geezer? This storm is going to blow everything away. If you stay here, there will be nothing left of you but a rocking chair and a pair of dentures," Barney argued.

"Then so be it. We all gotta go sometime."

"Okay. See if I care," said Barney. "I'm not ready to die yet. It's been nice knowing you, old man."

"Barney, I can't go." Eli explained. "Oh, you wouldn't understand. There's a point in life where you stop making memories and start living in them. All I am is my memories. I can't leave this house. This is where Mother and I raised our children. I just can't leave this old place. I *am* this old place."

With that, Barney walked over to Eli and quietly laid down at his feet. If Eli was going to die, Barney was going to go with him.

Back in the Rossini household, chaos reigned.

"Okay, you kids! Line up! Count off! We don't wanna forget nobody. Let's go!" shouted Angelo over the noise.

Finally, after lots of yelling and screaming, Angelo was able to line up the children, his wife, and the two talking dogs.

"All right, everybody. Move out! And stay in line!"

As the Rossini family moved outside, the wind picked up one of the children and carried him away. Angelo reached up and grabbed him by the pants, pulling him back to earth.

Gina was yelling, "The kids! They blowing everywhere!"

"That's it! Don't nobody blow anywhere! First kid to blow away gets his bottom spanked," shouted Angelo.

"Pap, I'm scared!" cried one of the children.

In the meantime, Al and Fredo were dragging little Tony by his diaper across the floor.

"You forgot one," said Al to Angelo as they stepped out the door. Just then another strong gust grabbed the baby and hurled him into the air. Al came to the rescue and pulled little Tony back down. Angelo didn't spank him; instead, he held him tighter.

Jon whistled as he casually packed a suitcase with a few of his favorite items.

"What are you doing?" Garfield cried.

"Oh, just packing a few things. Here's Mr. Toothbrush. I never go anywhere without him."

"Well, while you're at it, you might as well pack your blue suit. You want to look good at your funeral!"

Garfield was getting hysterical as the wind rattled the windows.

"Here. You better take this lamp! And this clock!" Garfield started throwing things at Jon.

"And this pillow and this glass and your baby pictures. And don't forget your precious bunny slippers!"

"Isn't there anything you're going to take, Garfield?"

"NO!" Garfield shouted. "Oh my gosh, yes. There is something!"

Garfield ran out of the room. When he returned he had Pooky in one paw and the refrigerator cord, with the refrigerator still attached, in his other paw.

Jon looked at Garfield and shook his head.

"Nice try, Garfield," Jon said, as Garfield reluctantly dropped the refrigerator cord.

Garfield, Odie and Jon ventured out into the storm. Leaning into a powerful head wind, the threesome pressed on.

They weren't alone. All around the neighborhood, houses emptied as pets and their owners headed in the direction of the theater.

Jon's journey was made more difficult by the weight of his suitcase, and just as he grabbed a tree to anchor himself to the ground, his suitcase blew open and all his belongings were carried away with the wind.

"My bunny slippers!" cried Jon. "Oh, no! And your dinner was in there, too!"

"This just isn't our day, is it, Odie?" Garfield asked, when Jon's underwear landed on his face.

In a nearby alley, the three strays, Bob, Lorenzo and Willard argued again.

"I think we should go to the old theater," stated Lorenzo.

"You think? *You think?* Who's the brains around here, Lorenzo?" asked Willard.

"I don't know. Who?" asked Lorenzo. With that, Willard smacked Lorenzo. Next, Willard smacked Bob.

"What did ya do that for, Willard?" asked Bob.

"I don't know. Just in case you had any stupid ideas floating around in that head," Willard replied.

"Don't worry. There's nothing in there," Bob said.

At the end of the alley sat an abandoned car. Willard spotted it and devised a plan.

"Okay, you guys, here's the plan. See that car? We're going to drive that car right out of this city. If we get moving, we can beat the storm."

"But, Willard, we don't know nothing about driving," Bob reminded him.

"Oh, it's easy," boasted Willard. "Bob, you get on the floor and push the pedals. Lorenzo, you steer. You mutts just do what I tell you and we'll be fine."

The three dogs ran down the alley and crawled in through the open windows.

"Okay, start the car."

"How do we do that?" asked Lorenzo.

Willard socked them both.

"Don't youse guys know anything?" asked Willard.

Eventually the three of them figured out how to start the car and soon it was swerving and jerking down the road, hitting fire hydrants, trash cans and everything else in the way.

"Turn left, Lorenzo!" Willard shouted.

"Uh, Willard? What's left?" Lorenzo asked.

The sound of screeching tires and screaming dogs filled the air.

Jon, Odie, and Garfield continued toward the theater, fighting rain, wind and flying debris every step of the way.

"Come on, boys. We're only a block away," shouted Jon over the storm.

"No problem! Wherever the wind goes, I go," Garfield replied.

As they neared the theater, a fiery bolt of lightning ripped through the sky, hitting a telephone pole and cracking it in two. The pole came crashing to the ground only inches away from Jon, Garfield and Odie. Wires snapped and sparks flew all around them.

"I guess this would be a bad time to stop and make a long-distance phone call," Garfield mused.

Still, they pressed on. Just as they had begun to breathe easier, a strong, spiraling wind picked up Garfield and carried him away. The gust hurled him down the street, tossing and turning him end over end.

SPLAT!

Garfield was pitched right into the stage door of the theater.

"This looks like my lucky day, after all," Garfield said, his back pressed against the door.

BLAT!

Odie came flying through the air, landing right smack on top of Garfield. Another second later, Jon flew into the scene, piling up on top of Garfield and Odie. The door blasted open and Jon, Garfield, and Odie soared into the theater, one after the other.

CRASH! SPLAT! BLAT!

"Well, that's one way to make an entrance," said Garfield.

After Garfield picked himself up and checked to see if he was all there, he scanned the theater to see who had escaped the storm.

Many of the neighborhood families had arrived. Garfield spotted Al, Fredo and the Rossini family. He saw several "Muffins" and their families, but he didn't see Barney and Eli. He scanned the room again and then, to his horror, realized that Arlene hadn't made it there either.

"Where's Arlene?" Garfield asked in a panic. "Didn't she make it back with her owner?"

"Don't you know, man?" Raoul answered. "Arlene doesn't have an owner. She's a stray, dude. An alley cat."

Garfield started for the stage door. He knew what he had to do. There was no time to waste. He struggled with the door and forced his way back outside into the horrible storm that was now engulfing the town.

"Arlene! Arlene!" Garfield shouted.

His voice could barely be heard over the howling storm. At the end of the street, a huge funnel cloud roared into view.

Just in front of the twister, a banged-up car came zooming around the corner. In it sat Bob, Willard, and Lorenzo, eyes wide and mouths open. Garfield could hear the dogs yelling at each other as the car ripped past him and disappeared around the corner.

"Arlene!" Garfield cried.

Out of the corner of his eye, Garfield noticed a tail sticking out from under a box in the corner of the alley. He approached the box and lifted it, not knowing what he'd find. Then his smile returned. Under the box, hiding from the storm, was his good friend, Arlene.

Garfield grabbed Arlene's paw and pulled her behind him as they headed out of the alley.

"We'll never make it, Garfield," said Arlene.

"Yes, we will," Garfield replied confidently.

Garfield was more determined than ever. He picked up a trash can and dumped the garbage on the ground.

"Get in," commanded Garfield.

Arlene reluctantly crawled into the dirty can. Once inside, Garfield and Arlene began rocking the can from side to side. When the can was in motion the two cats braced themselves for a bumpy ride. A moment later, thanks to the tornado, they were airborne.

"It's not first class, but it'll have to do," said Garfield to Arlene.

"Well, it certainly is an inexpensive way to travel," replied Arlene. "I can't say much for the in-flight movie, though."

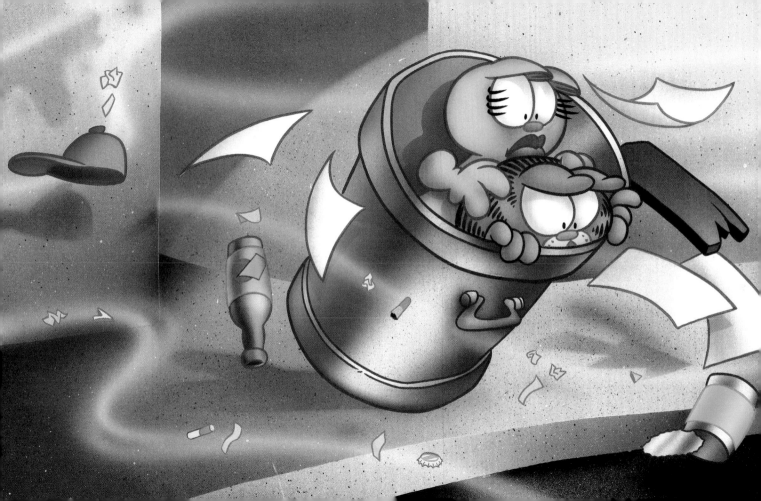

The storm had reached the peak of its fury. Inside the whirling trash can, Garfield and Arlene held on for their lives. Even though they tried to joke, they knew they were in grave danger.

Garfield and the other neighborhood animals had been right. It certainly was the worst storm they'd ever seen. Windows shattered, buildings rattled, and debris filled the air as the dark funnel cloud ripped through the town.

BANG!

The trash can carrying Garfield and Arlene smashed into a telephone pole and came crashing to the ground. It teetered back and forth and then became still.

Slowly, dizzily, Garfield and Arlene emerged from the can.

"That's the worst landing I've ever seen," said Garfield.

"I've seen worse," said Arlene. She took Garfield's paw and squeezed it tightly. Garfield led her toward the theater. The stage door was now in view.

"Run!" yelled Garfield.

The words had barely left his lips when another blustery rush of wind swept them off their feet. The next thing they knew their faces were plastered against the stage door.

"I'm getting real tired of this," said Garfield.

Inside, Jon heard two thuds against the door.

"What was that?" he wondered, pulling the door open. In flew Garfield and Arlene, the tornado on their heels.

Jon had no sooner forced the door closed, when several shards of glass pierced the door like so many daggers. The old theater began to shake and quiver. Windows shattered. Water pipes burst. They felt a sudden change in the air pressure as the roof began to creak. Everyone in the theater, pets and all, looked up in horror and watched as the roof was torn away from the building.

Blackness fell upon them.

After what seemed like an eternity, the debris on the theater floor began to move.

First Garfield, and then Arlene, emerged. They grasped each other's paws tightly. They could hear moaning all over the room.

"YIP! YIP! YIP!" came a sound from the floor.

Garfield and Arlene looked over at the sound. It was Odie. He was lying in a shallow puddle, his paws covering his eyes.

Garfield grabbed him by the ears and lifted him out of the little puddle while Odie continued whining.

"Odie, you're okay, boy. Look, it's all right. You're alive," said Garfield to his frightened friend.

Odie peeked out from his paws. When he saw Garfield and Arlene standing over him, he smiled and wagged his tail. "Yeah, I know, boy. I love you, too," said Garfield, giving him a hug.

"Garfield! Odie! We're alive!" Jon rejoiced.

All around them, pets and their owners emerged from the wreckage. There were bruises and cuts, but miraculously, no one was badly hurt.

Garfield could feel the relief in the room as the crowd realized that they had survived the ordeal.

"We're alive! Whoopee! Let's eat," thought Garfield.

"Garfield, I'm so proud of you. Not only did you save Arlene, but you saved my life, too. How will I ever repay you?" asked Jon, hugging and squeezing his pets.

"A cash reward comes to mind," thought Garfield.

"Garfield, speak to me. We have so much to talk about," said Jon.

Garfield looked at Jon, confused.

"Garfield, talk to me. I know you can do it! I heard you. What about our career in show business?" pleaded Jon.

Garfield shrugged his shoulders.

"Was I dreaming? Am I nuts?" cried Jon.

Garfield just smiled. The pets had accomplished what they set out to do and they all knew it was time to act like pets again.

Down the street from the theater, or what remained of the theater, Eli's house lay flattened by the storm. Eli stood, bent over the rubble, searching for his faithful friend, Barney.

He sifted through the ruins carefully until he came upon the motionless body of Barney.

"Barney, darn your hide. Do something! Don't you dare die on me now. Who's going to wake me in the morning? Who's going to growl at me when I forget to turn the TV off at night?"

Barney didn't react.

."Forget what I said about the memories, Barney. My memories are scattered all over this end of the county by now. Hang the memories! Hang everything, Barney. You're the most important thing in the world to me, ol' boy," Eli cried.

Eli hung his head, tears streaming down his wrinkled old face. Barney raised his head and licked the tears away.

"Barney! Why, you mangy, old cur! You were playing possum with me, weren't you? You ol' devil! Boy, am I glad to see you!"

Eli hugged Barney tightly, then kissed him on the nose.

Even though the storm had wreaked havoc on the town, some good things happened that day. For one, a nice lady took Arlene home to live with her and her cat named Muffin, and the Rossini family returned to their home to find it damaged only slightly and with a new appreciation for Al and Fredo. They knew Al and Fredo could be counted on to keep their family safe.

Some of the dogs named Spot had taken the opportunity to complain to their owners about the names they had been given. Consequently, there were now dogs in the neighborhood with new, more distinguished names like William, James, Jonathan, and Throckmorton.

When Jon, Garfield, and Odie reached their home, they were amazed to see it still standing.

"Will you look at that! This must be some sort of miracle!" exclaimed Jon.

Just then, they heard a rattling, clanking, clattering noise in the street. They turned to see Lorenzo, Willard, and Bob sitting behind the wheel of what was once a car. As the car came to a halt, the front and back bumpers dropped off. Then the car doors, the hood, and the trunk fell to the ground. Lorenzo, Willard and Bob sat in the street, the entire car a shambles. Lorenzo still had the steering wheel tightly clenched in his paws.

Jon turned back to open his front door. As he turned the doorknob to enter, the house began to shudder and creak. First the left wall of the house collapsed. Then, the right wall came down. As the front and back of the house began to cave in, Jon just stood, the doorknob in his hand and his mouth agape.

"My home! My castle! What next?" cried Jon.

Garfield approached, holding the door handle to the refrigerator in his paw.

"My home! My castle!" thought Garfield.

Jon and Garfield laughed and hugged each other hard. They knew the house and refrigerator could both be replaced. The only really important thing, their friendship, had survived the storm, and that made them both feel very, very, lucky.

STRIPS, SPECIALS OR BESTSELLING BOOKS. . .
GARFIELD'S ON EVERYONE'S MENU

Don't miss even one episode in the Tubby Tabby's hilarious series!

BY: JIM DAVIS

__GARFIELD AT LARGE (#1)   32013/$6.95
__GARFIELD GAINS WEIGHT (#2)   32008/$6.95
__GARFIELD BIGGER THAN LIFE (#3)   32007/$6.95
__GARFIELD WEIGHS IN (#4)   32010/$6.95
__GARFIELD TAKES THE CAKE (#5))   32009/$6.95
__GARFIELD EATS HIS HEART OUT (#6)   32018/$6.95
__GARFIELD SITS AROUND THE HOUSE (#7)   32011/$6.95
__GARFIELD TIPS THE SCALES (#8)   33580/$6.95
__GARFIELD LOSES HIS FEET (#9)   31805/$6.95
__GARFIELD MAKE IT BIG (#10)   31928/$6.95
__GARFIELD ROLLS ON (#11)   32634/$6.95
__GARFIELD OUT TO LUNCH (#12)   33118/$6.95
__GARFIELD FOOD FOR THOUGHT(#13)   34129/$6.95

__GARFIELD SWALLOWS HIS PRIDE (#14)   34725/$6.95
__GARFIELD WORLDWIDE (#15)   35158/$6.95
__GARFIELD ROUNDS OUT (#16)   35388/$6.95
__GARFIELD CHEWS THE FAT (#17)   35956/$6.95
__GARFIELD GOES TO WAIST (#18)   36430/$6.95

GARFIELD AT HIS SUNDAY BEST!
__GARFIELD TREASURY   33106/$9.95
__THE SECOND GARFIELD TREASURY   33276/$10.95
__THE THIRD GARFIELD TREASURY   32635/$9.95
__THE FOURTH GARFIELD TREASURY   34726/$10.95
__THE FIFTH GARFIELD TREASURY   36268/$9.95

BALLANTINE SALES
Dept. TA, 201 E. 50th St., New York, N.Y. 10022

Please send me the BALLANTINE BOOKS I have checked above. I am enclosing $ .... (add $2.00 for the first book and 50¢ for each additional book to cover postage and handling). Send check or money order—no cash or C.O.D.'s please. Prices are subject to change without notice.

Name _____

Address _____

City_____ State_____ Zip Code_____
30   Allow at least 4 weeks for delivery   3/90 TA-135